Brilliant Support Activities

Sentence Level Work

Irene Yates

Brilliant Publications

We hope you and your class enjoy using this book. Other books in the series include:

Language titles

Word Level Work – Phonics	978 1 897675 32 8
Word Level Work – Vocabulary	978 1 903853 07 8
Text Level Work	978 1 903853 00 9

Science titles

Understanding Living Things	978 1 897675 59 5
Understanding Materials	978 1 897675 60 1
Understanding Physical Processes	978 1 897675 61 8

Published by Brilliant Publications
www.brilliantpublications.co.uk

Sales
BEBC (Brilliant Publications)
Albion Close, Parkstone, Poole, Dorset BH12 3LL, UK
Tel: 01202 712910   Fax: 0845 1309300

Editorial
Brilliant Publications
Unit 10, Sparrow Hall Farm, Edlesborough, Dunstable LU6 2ES, UK

The name Brilliant Publications and its logo are registered trade marks.

Written by Irene Yates
Cover designed by Small World Design
Illustrated by Lynda Murray

Printed in the UK

© Irene Yates 2001
First published in 2001, reprinted 2008.
10 9 8 7 6 5 4 3 2
ISBN 978 1 897675 33 5

Contents

Introduction to the series

The Brilliant Support Activities series contains four language titles designed to give reinforcement to pupils who are finding it difficult to keep up with the skills and concepts in the National Literacy Strategy. The four books are closely linked:

- Word Level Work – Vocabulary
- Word Level Work – Phonics
- Sentence Level Work
- Text Level Work

Each book contains 42 photocopiable ideas for use with Key Stage 2 pupils who are working at levels consistent with the first four years of the National Literacy Strategy document. The activities are presented in an age-appropriate manner and provide a flexible, but structured, resource for teaching pupils to understand all the concepts that are introduced in the Literacy Hour during reception, Y1, Y2 and Y3.

The tasks in the books are kept short and snappy, to facilitate concentration. The vocabulary used is especially focused on the lists of high frequency and medium frequency words that the children are to be taught as sight recognition words during the National Literacy Strategy. The pages have a clear layout and the text has been kept to a minimum so that struggling readers can cope. To ensure that the instructions are easy to follow, the following logos have been used to indicate different types of activity:

 What to do

 Think and do

 Read

 Help

Many pupils begin to feel disaffected when they find abstract language concepts hard to grasp. The activities in this series are designed, with information and questioning, to foster understanding and to help those pupils to experience success and achievement. The expectation that the pupil will achieve will help to build confidence, competence and self-esteem which, in turn, will foster learning.

Introduction to the book

The activity pages are designed to support and consolidate the work you do during the Literacy Hour. They are intended to add to your pupils' knowledge of the different concepts that are introduced during the first four years.

Many of the concepts of syntax and punctuation that are met in the National Literacy Strategy Sentence Level work are quite abstract; they sometimes require lots of reinforcement before they are understood and made functional. The tasks in this book are designed to supplement and reinforce these concepts, in order to build up the children's confidence and knowledge of the English language.

The sheets can be used with individual children, pairs or very small groups, as the need arises. The text on the pages has been kept as short as possible, so that reluctant or poorer readers will not feel swamped by 'words on the page'. For the same reason we have used white space, boxes and logos, to help the pupils to understand the sheets easily, and to give them a measure of independence in working through them.

It is not the author's intention that a teacher should expect all the children to complete all the sheets. Rather that the sheets be used with a flexible approach, so that the book will provide a bank of resources that will meet needs as they arise. Many of the sheets can be modified and extended in very simple ways.

Lots of letters

Read

THESE ARE CAPITAL LETTERS:

A B C D E F G H I J K L M N O P Q R S T U V W X Y Z

What to do

Write these words in small letters.

BOY ___boy___   COMPUTER _____

GIRL _____   TELEVISION _____

SCHOOL _____   VIDEO _____

FOOTBALL _____   DISCO _____

RABBIT _____   RAIN _____

Write these words in capital letters:

swim _____   run _____

sport _____   leap _____

playing _____   kick _____

game _____   throw _____

jump _____   hit _____

Help

CAPITAL LETTERS are sometimes called UPPER CASE LETTERS.
Small letters are sometimes called lower case letters.

Capital letters and lower case letters

Read

CAPITAL LETTERS ARE LIKE THIS.

Lower case letters are like this.

What to do

Write a whole sentence in capital letters:

Write the sentence again in lower case letters:

(Remember the first letter of a sentence has to be a capital letter. What do you need at the end of each sentence?)

Think and do

Write four more short sentences in capital letters.

1

2

3

4

Now write them again in lower case letters.

1

2

3

4

Help

CAPITAL LETTERS are sometimes called upper case letters.
Lower case letters are sometimes called small letters.

© Irene Yates
Sentence Level Work

What to do

To do this game you need a dictionary.

Write the letters of the alphabet down the side of the page.
The first three are done for you.

Use the dictionary to find one word for each letter.
Try to look for new words. Make them interesting.

Copy the spelling exactly.

A

B

C

Dictionary puzzle 1

Read

A dictionary is useful to tell you what words mean.
The words are all in alphabetical order.

These words are in alphabetical order, starting at A.
Read the words and their meanings.

atlas	a book of maps
bear	a large wild animal
clothes	things we wear
different	not the same
eyes	what we see with
first	at the front
great	good, or big
happy	feeling good
inside	within, not outside
jigsaw	a puzzle with pieces that fit together
knowledge	what you know
light	not dark
morning	the beginning of the day

What to do

Use the words to do this puzzle:

1
2
3
4
5
6
7
8
9
10
11
12
13

Clues

Within, not outside

A book of maps

What we see with

Feeling good

What you know

Things we wear

Good, or big

The beginning of the day

A puzzle with pieces that fit together

At the front

Not the same

Not dark

A large, wild animal

Read

A dictionary is useful to tell you what words mean.
The words are all in alphabetical order.

These words are in alphabetical order, starting at N.
Read the words and their meanings.

number	tells you how many
outside	not inside
place	a special space
quiet	not noisy
right	not wrong, or left
sometimes	not all the time
today	now, not yesterday or tomorrow
under	beneath or below
voice	what you speak with
whole	all of something
xylophone	a musical instrument
your	belongs to you
zipper	a fastener

What to do

Use the words to do this puzzle:

1
2
3
4
5
6
7
8
9
10
11
12
13

Clues

Not inside

Beneath or below

Belongs to you

A fastener

What you speak with

Tells you how many

Not wrong, or left

All of something

A special space

Now, not yesterday or tomorrow

A musical instrument

Not noisy

Not all the time

What to do

Here are the meanings of some words. The words are in alphabetical order. The first word begins with K, the last begins with T.

What are the words? Fit them into the puzzle.

		Clues
1	K _ _ _	Something you do with your foot
2	L _ _ _ _ _	The capital of England
3	M _ _ _ _ _	A place to buy bargains
4	N _ _ _ _ _ _ _ _ _	A kind of toad
5	O _ _ _ _ _	A juicy kind of fruit
6	P _ _ _ _ _	More than one person
7	Q _ _ _ _ _ _	Something you ask
8	R _ _ _ _ _	A furry animal
9	S _ _ _ _ _ _	Catch a train here
10	T _ _ _ _	You do it inside your head

Think and do

Make up ten word puzzles of your own, starting at A and ending with J.

Clues

1

2

3

4

5

6

7

8

9

10

© Irene Yates
Sentence Level Work

What to do

Here are the meanings of some words. The words are in alphabetical order. The first word begins with T, the last begins with Z.

What are the words? Fit them into the puzzle.

Clues

1 T _ _ _   Go round

2 U _ _ _   Second-hand

3 V _ _ _ _   Part of a poem or song

4 W _ _ _ _   In which place?

5 X _ _ _   Shows the inside of the body

6 Y _ _ _   Twelve months

7 Z _ _ _ _   An African animal

Think and do

Look in the dictionary. Make up a puzzle of your own for the last six letters of the alphabet.

Clues

1

2

3

4

5

6

Read

Adjectives are words that tell you what someone or something is like. Adjectives describe things. These words are all adjectives.

They are all words to describe this monster.

What to do

Write five adjectives each to describe these:

An alien	Your favourite food
A bike	School

Your best friend

Describe it!

What to do

Choose one of these:

Your best friend · Your mum or dad · School · Your favourite clothes · Your favourite game · A pet or animal

Write five adjectives to describe it.

My choice:

My adjectives:

Think and do

Use your adjectives to write five sentences about your choice.

1

2

3

4

5

Read

Adjectives are words which tell you what someone or something is like.

Here are two lists of adjectives. The words are the opposites of each other. For example, big is the opposite of little. But they are in the wrong order.

Read all the words carefully.

big	tall
heavy	gentle
wet	uncomfortable
short	little
narrow	hot
dirty	dry
huge	light
fierce	clean
comfortable	small
cold	wide

What to do

Make two lists here, putting the opposites in the correct places.

big	little
_____	_____
_____	_____
_____	_____
_____	_____
_____	_____
_____	_____
_____	_____
_____	_____
_____	_____

Help

Words that mean the opposite of other words are called 'antonyms'.

Which adjective?

Read

Here is a list of adjectives:

tallest   huge   bigger

red   dangerous   sunny

What to do

Write the adjective that fits into each sentence.

1   Elephants are _____ animals.

2   Today is a _____ day.

3   I'm wearing my _____ jumper.

4   The _____ animal is the giraffe.

5   Dinosaurs are _____ than mice.

6   Is a busy road _____ ?

Think and do

Can you put the adjectives into alphabetical order?

Help

Adjectives are words that tell you what something is like.
They describe things.

Read

Dogs can be:

◆ noisy

◆ greedy

◆ muddy

◆ friendly

◆ big

◆ small

What to do

Give six adjectives of your own for:

Boys can be:

◆

◆

◆

◆

◆

◆

Girls can be:

◆

◆

◆

◆

◆

◆

Games can be:

◆

◆

◆

◆

◆

◆

Help

Adjectives are words that tell you what something is like.
They describe things.

Naming things

Read

The words that give things names are called nouns.

			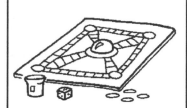
Carrot	**Car**	**Teacher**	**Game**
is the name of an orange vegetable.	is the name of something you drive.	is the name of a person who teaches.	is the name of something you play.

What to do

Write sentences like these for the following nouns.

Daisy is the name of

Trumpet

Jacket

Ant

Book

Dog

Skateboard

Home

Spoon

Cereal

Which group?

What to do

Here are 15 nouns, or naming words.
They fit into three groups:

Something you wear   Something you eat   Something you play with
      (Clothes)   (Food)   (Toys or games)

Put the nouns into the correct groups.

Cabbage   Peas   Action man
Football   Computer   Jam
Jeans   Bread   Shirt
Pear   Pasta   Truck
Skateboard   Socks   Beans

**Something you eat
(Food)**

**Something you wear
(Clothes)**

**Something you play with
(Toys or games)**

Read

Here is an elephant:

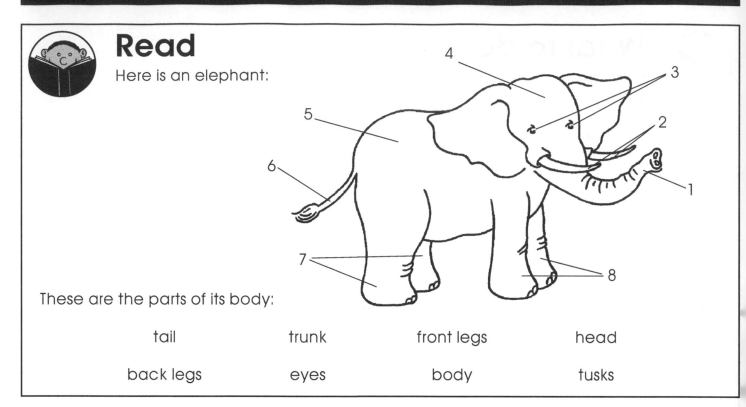

These are the parts of its body:

tail	trunk	front legs	head
back legs	eyes	body	tusks

What to do

Write a sentence explaining each number, like this:

1   **This is the elephant's trunk.**

2

3

4

5

6

7

8

 ## Help

Don't forget the apostrophe! It is there to show that the different parts belong to the elephant.

Read

Here is a car:

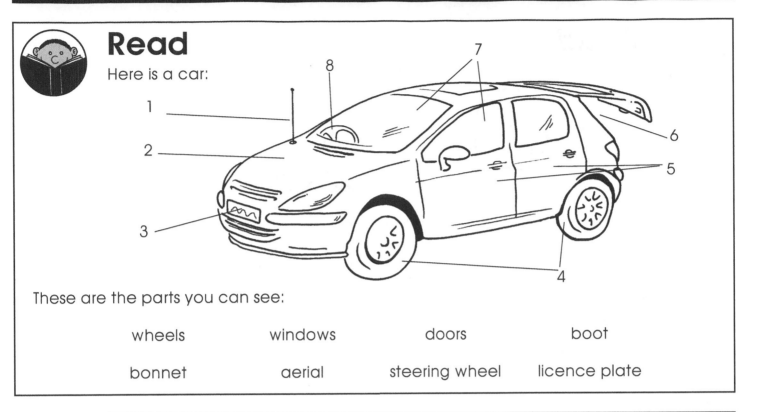

These are the parts you can see:

wheels	windows	doors	boot
bonnet	aerial	steering wheel	licence plate

What to do

Write a sentence explaining each number, like this:

1 **This is the car's aerial.**

2

3

4

5

6

7

8

Help

Don't forget the apostrophe! It is there to show that the different parts belong to the car.

Beetle words

Read

This is how to draw a beetle. It has:

one body   one head   two eyes

two feelers   six legs    one tail

What to do

For each word you can read and write, you may choose one piece of the beetle to draw.

There are 13 pieces altogether.

Read

then	tree	new
but	man	saw
than	here	if
very	many	your
after		

Beetle

Write

Write sentences, using as many of the words as you can. Score 2 points for each word. Can you get 26 points?

Help

You can use as many words as you like in each sentence.

Alien words

Read

This is how to draw an alien. It has:

one body

two heads

four eyes

three legs

two attenae

one flashing light

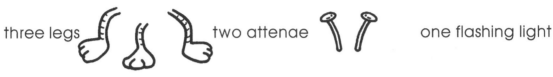

What to do

For each word you can read and write, you may choose one piece of the alien to draw.

There are 13 pieces altogether.

Read

way	with	here
old	over	laugh
too	out	seen
from	us	him
take		

Alien

Write

Write sentences, using as many of the words as you can. Score 2 points for each word. Can you get 26 points?

Help

You can use as many words as you like in each sentence.

Colour words

Read

These words tell you the names of colours:

green	orange	blue	pink
black	grey	yellow	red
brown	purple		

What to do

Write each word here, in its own colour:

blue   red

pink   purple

yellow   brown

grey   orange

black   green

Think and do

Colour the flower pink.   Colour the ball orange.

Colour the cow brown.   Colour the bus red.

Colour the dog black.   Colour the sun yellow.

Colour the car green.   Colour the cat grey.

Colour the T-shirt purple.   Colour the leaf green.

Days of the week

Read

There are seven days in a week.
They are:

first	1st	Sunday
second	2nd	Monday
third	3rd	Tuesday
fourth	4th	Wednesday
fifth	5th	Thursday
sixth	6th	Friday
seventh	7th	Saturday

What to do

Fill in these columns:

		2nd
Tuesday		
	sixth	

Think and do

Write sentences about the days of the week here.
Use the words: first, then, after that, last.

Read

A noun is the name of something. Look at these nouns:

 boy
 Tom
 America
 wasp

Can you see the difference? Two of them start with capital letters. This is beause they are proper nouns. They have capital letters to tell you that the names are special.

- ◆ Names of people are proper nouns.
- ◆ Names of towns and cities are proper nouns.
- ◆ Names of countries are proper nouns.
- ◆ Names of day and months are proper nouns.

What to do

Put in the first letter of these proper nouns.

Choose from:

F M T H T B S W S K S J N J M A D W S L R

Boys' names	Girls' names	Days
__ iam	__ nn	__ uesday
__ ack	__ aureen	__ aturday
__ arry	__ ikki	__ hursday
__ ames	__ ate	__ onday
__ am	__ asha	__ ednesday
__ yan	__ endy	__ unday
__ anny	__ ella	__ riday

Read

A proper noun is a special noun. 'Proper' means 'own special'.

You might be a boy (noun),
but your own special name
might be Tom (proper noun).

You might be a girl (noun),
but your own special name
might be Jo (proper noun).

Proper nouns begin with a capital letter.

What to do

Draw lines to match these proper nouns with what they are.

1	February	a city
2	Everest	a boy's name
3	Edinburgh	a girl's name
4	Roald Dahl	a country
5	Jack	a month
6	Mrs Smith	an island
7	Sunday	a mountain
8	Jane	an author
9	Isle of Wight	a day
10	Spain	a teacher

What to do

Make a list of verbs in alphabetical order:

add

beat

catch

Think and do

Use a dictionary to check your spellings. Give yourself
two points for every word you've got correct. How many
points have you got?

Verbs

Read

The words that are underlined say what you do. They are words for doing things. They are called verbs. Every complete sentence must have a verb.

Can you <u>read</u>?   The verb is __read__ .

Do you <u>play</u> football?   The verb is _____ .

Can you <u>swim</u>?   The verb is _____ .

Do you <u>sleep</u>?   The verb is _____ .

Can you <u>sing</u>?   The verb is _____ .

Do you <u>eat</u>?   The verb is _____ .

What to do

Here are some verbs:

| went | painted | made | drank |
| laughed | talked | jumped | ran |

Write a sentence for each verb, like this:

1 Yesterday I <u>went</u> to school.

2

3

4

5

6

7

8

Help

Don't forget the capital letter and full stop for a proper sentence!

This sheet may be photocopied for use by the purchasing institution only.
www.brilliantpublications.co.uk

Read

All of these words are part of the same verb:

go   going   gone

What to do

Can you put these verbs together?

There are three words for each verb. Cross out each set of three as you find them.

drawing   drew   saying

~~ran~~   fly   painting

paint   ~~running~~   had   wrote

having

singing   writing   said

write

painted   flew

sung   have

~~run~~   draw

say

flying   sing

Fill in the chart:

run	running	ran

Read

The noun dog means one dog.

The noun cat means one cat.

The noun dogs means more than one dog.

Which letter has changed the word? _____

To make a noun mean more than one we often add an 's'.

What to do

Make these words plural:

1   adventure   _____

2   boy   _____

3   coat   _____

4   den   _____

5   elephant   _____

6   frog   _____

7   goat   _____

8   hen   _____

9   ice-cream   _____

10 jig   _____

11 king   _____

12 lamb   _____

13 mop   _____

Make these words singular:

1   names   _____

2   oaks   _____

3   pains   _____

4   queens   _____

5   rabbits   _____

6   sacks   _____

7   tables   _____

8   uncles   _____

9   vests   _____

10 words   _____

11 xylophones   _____

12 yawns   _____

13 zigzags   _____

Help

The word for one is 'singular'. The word for more than one is 'plural'.

This sheet may be photocopied for use by the purchasing institution only.
www.brilliantpublications.co.uk

Read

If a singular noun ends with a hissing sound – like 'box' – we have to add 'es' to make it plural.

Like this: singular = box

plural = boxes

What to do

Make these hissing words plural by adding 'es'.
Write out the words in your best handwriting.

watch

fox

glass

fish

dish

match

peach

church

kiss

buzz

six

bench

bus

porch

pass

Careful handwriting helps you learn to spell.

Help

Remember, singular = one, plural = more than one.

A hissing sound could be 'ch', 'tch', 'sh', 'x' or 's'.

Changing a 'y'

Read

Some singular words end with 'y'.

If the letter before the 'y' is a vowel, you just add as 's'.

Singular	Plural
monkey	monkeys
donkey	donkeys

If the letter before the 'y' is a consonant, you must change the 'y' into 'ie' and then add 's'.

Singular	Plural
baby	babies
country	countries
spy	spies

What to do

Make these words plural. Use your best handwriting.

fly   _____

story   _____

pony   _____

fairy   _____

city   _____

sky   _____

army   _____

factory   _____

Careful handwriting helps you learn to spell.

What's a question?

Read

A question is a sentence that asks something. It must begin with a capital letter and end with a question mark.

What to do

Here are six questions.

Answer the questions. Make sure you write proper sentences for your answers.

How old are you?

Who is your best friend?

What is your favourite TV programme?

Why do you like it?

When do you watch it?

Where do you play on Saturdays?

Think and do

Write five questions of your own:

How _____

Who _____

What _____

When _____

Where _____

(Don't forget the question marks!)

Help a friend to answer your questions.

Read

A question asks something. It has a question mark, like this **?**, at the end of it.
An answer tells something. It has a full stop, like this **.**, at the end of it.

What to do

Answer the questions. Don't forget the full stops.

What is this?	It is a	
What is this?	It is a	
What is this? 		
What is this?		
What is this?		
What is this?		
What are these?	They are	
What are these?	They	
What are these?		
What are these?		
What are these?		
What are these?		
What are these?		
What are these?		

This sheet may be photocopied for use by the purchasing institution only.
www.brilliantpublications.co.uk

Read

Remember, a question has a **?** (question mark) at the end of it.
An answer does not have a question mark.

What to do

Read a question in List 1. Find the answer for it in List 2.
Write out the question and its proper answer.

List 1 – Questions

Is football a game?
Is school a place?
Are people human?
Who is in charge of the class?
Do trees grow?
Can a computer think?
Do cars have wings?
Are shoes and boots the same?

List 2 – Answers

A teacher is in charge.
No, it can't think.
Yes, they grow.
Yes, it's a game.
No, they do not.
Yes, they are human.
No, they are not.
Yes, it's a place.

Think and do

Write three questions of your own. Get your friend to write the answers.

1

2

3

Did you remember the question marks?

This sheet may be photocopied for use by the purchasing institution only
www.brilliantpublications.co.u

Can you answer these yourself?

Read

Questions are sentences, too. They must begin with a capital letter and end with a question mark instead of a full stop.

What to do

Read these questions. Write your own answers beside them.
Remember to write your answers in proper sentences.

1   Are you a girl or a boy?

2   What is your full name?

3   Where do you live?

4   What colour is your hair?

5   What colour are your eyes?

6   Who is your best friend?

7   What is your favourite lesson?

8   What is your favourite TV programme?

9   How old are you?

10 When is your birthday?

Think and do

Can you write your own address?
If so, write it here.

Can you write the address of your school? If so, write it here.

What to do

Read these sentences. Each one is the answer to a question. Write what you think the questions are beside them.

Remember to write your questions in proper sentences with a capital letter to begin and a question mark to end.

1   New York is in America.   **Where is New York?**

2   It is London.

3   I will be 10 next year.

4   It is the day after Christmas Day.

5   We have break-time at 10.30.

6   I stay at school for my lunch.

7   We play in the playground.

8   It takes half an hour to get to school.

9   Robots can't swim.

10 There are no more questions.

Think and do

Write three more answers. Ask your friend to read them. What does your friend think the questions must be?

1

2

3

Sound puzzle

Read

Some words sound the same but they do not always look the same.

They do not mean the same thing.

Help

Words than sound the same but look different and mean different things are called homonyms (say hom-on-ims).

What to do

Draw lines to join these homonyms together.

1	bare	eight
2	blew	high
3	for	fur
4	hi	here
5	flour	bear
6	break	herd
7	bread	serial
8	ate	buy
9	groan	fare
10	hear	blue
11	hole	bred
12	fir	sell
13	know	flower
14	heard	grown
15	fair	whole
16	cereal	four
17	be	no
18	by	brake
19	cell	hare
20	hair	bee

What to do

Make a sentence for each letter of the alphabet, like this:

A   is for ant.   N _____

B   is for bed.   O _____

C   is for cave.   P _____

D   is for _____   Q _____

E _____   R _____

F _____   S _____

G _____   T _____

H _____   U _____

I _____   V _____

J _____   W _____

K _____   X _____

L _____   Y _____

M _____   Z _____

You may choose your own words, or take them from this list:

animal	friend	know	place	today	x-ray
birthday	garden	light	quick	under	year
clothes	head	money	round	very	zebra
different	inside	number	something	window	
eyes	jump	often			

Think and do

Can you read all the words in the list?

Proper sentences

Read

Read these words:

said	like	look	play	away
they	going	come	went	was

What to do

Write five proper sentences. They can be statements or questions. Use any two of the words in each sentence. Score 2 points for each word you use.

Think and do

Have you scored 20 points? If not, try again!

Help

Don't forget capital letters and full stops.

Read

Read these words:

could	about	don't	now	help
must	what	next	push	these

What to do

Write five proper sentences. They can be statements or questions. Use any two of the words in each sentence. Score 2 points for each word you use.

Think and do

Have you scored 20 points? If not, try again!

Help

Don't forget capital letters and full stops.

Use the words

Read

Read these words:

again	another	want	more	over
good	should	home	who	last

What to do

Write five proper sentences. They can be statements or questions. Use any two of the words in each sentence. Score 2 points for each word you use.

Think and do

Have you scored 20 points? If not, try again!

Help

Don't forget capital letters and full stops.

Read

Read these words:

because	make	little	two	our
some	where	down	been	their

What to do

Write five proper sentences. They can be statements or questions. Use any two of the words in each sentence. Score 2 points for each word you use.

Think and do

Have you scored 20 points? If not, try again!

Help

Don't forget capital letters and full stops.

What to do

Read these sentences. There is something wrong with them.

Write them out again, properly.

1   which season comes after summer

2   when do the leaves fall from the trees

3   sometimes it rains

4   the weather can change very quickly

5   when do you need your wellington boots

6   bees collect pollen from flowers

7   do birds like honey

8   don't pick the flowers

9   how deep is the snow

10 can you make a snowman

Help

Think about capital letters, full stops and question marks.

Exclamation!

What to do

Read the sentences below. They are not finished properly because they do not have punctuation marks at the end.

Copy out eight sentences that you think show surprise or give an order. Put the exclamation mark in.

1   Help

2   Give that to me

3   How dare you

4   Shall we go for a walk

5   Call the police

6   I've just finished reading my book

7   The party was fantastic

8   Did you have a good time

9   Ouch

10 Wow

11 It wasn't me

12 The sun is shining

1

2

3

4

5

6

7

8

Put the appropriate punctuation mark at the end of each of the four sentences that are left.

Help

When you show surprise it can be humour, joy, anger, fear, pain or danger.

Read

Speech marks show you words that are spoken. They always appear in pairs " " – one set to begin a speech, one set to end it.

For example:

Ayesha said she would like a drink of water.

Ayesha said, "I would like a drink of water."

What to do

Change these sentences so that they have direct speech.

Tom said it has been a good match.

_____

Bella decided to go out and play.

_____

Lisa wanted her hair cut.

_____

Manesh said she was cold.

_____

More talking

Read

Notice where the speech marks are in these sentences:

Jack said, "How are you?"

"Keep your cool," said the lion.

"I'm cold," whispered the princess.

What to do

Make up some speech to finish these sentences.
Don't forget the " " marks and other punctuation.

_____ asked Tom.

The teacher said, _____

_____ cried the boy.

Somebody whispered, _____

_____ said Dad.

The alien screeched, _____

Help

There must always be a punctuation mark inside the speech marks.

Lightning Source UK Ltd.
Milton Keynes UK
UKOW07f1806120616

276085UK00003B/68/P

9 781897 675335